NATIONAL GEOGRAPHIC

T0044889

Using Your Senses at School

Jalmin Sweeney-Blight

You can use your senses at school.

CAUTION
3

What can you see at school?

a classroom

a gym

a library

What can you hear at school?

children singing

a teacher talking

a ball bouncing

What can you feel at school?

a smooth desk

a soft teddy bear

a heavy bag

What can you smell at school?

flowers

a marker

food

What can you taste at school?

Lunch!